Gardens for the Senses

Gardens for the Senses

The Spanish Gardens of Javier Mariátegui

Edition Axel Menges

ISBN 978-3-936681-98-7

Second, unrevised edition

Printing and binding: Graspo CZ, a. s., Zlín, Czech Republic

Texts: Javier Mariátegui Valdés
Translation into English: Alberto Calderón González
Proof reading: Richard Grant
Photography: Javier Mariátegui Valdés, Casilda Mariátegui, Mark Bentley
Photo editing: Alejandro Brañas
Drawings: Javier Mariátegui Valdés
Book design: Covadonga Blasco Veganzones
Jacket design: Axel Menges

Dedicated to

my mother
origin and inspiration

Guillermo and Ana
patrons and conceivers
of dreams

Ángel Gil
a loyal friend

Juan Luis Líbano
an indispensable source
of imagination

**and all those whose efforts
helped to create
each of the gardens**

... Just gardens

Light; the melodious murmur of water; views; scents; the blending of modern and classical; order; dramatic effects; the impact of a single vista; reflections on water, and its subtle motion; nature and order intermingled; the flowers of my childhood – all of these have formed the guidelines of my garden designs, of which, here, I present a small sample.

In each of them I have sought to adapt to the landscape, to the buildings, to the client, and to my perception of what the genius loci, the spirit of the place, called for. These gardens are the dishes created from such ingredients.

Led by passion and by a willingness to always try something new for each of them, I have often walked through paths in the dark, whose destination I could not initially ascertain. After an initial fear, results always came as a surprise – as though in a poem, things appeared that I had not realised were there.

I am lucky to have had clients who taught me to see gardens from a different perspective; who guided me along the way; who knew what they wanted but not how it could be achieved. There I just added my small contribution, and their garden – my garden – became the outcome of a host of intervening ideas and people: owners, interior decorators, contractors, friends in the gardening com pany, office colleagues and, at the end of the line, I, the gardener, drawing from here and there to achieve something in harmony with the landscape.

Most of these gardens are in the countryside, set within sweeping, overwhelming landscapes, where the garden should be the frame that will attach value to such a display. I just added the frame … for my idea was that these should not be "signature" gardens, but gardens perfectly tailored to that place.

I feel obliged to thank all of those who have entrusted me with their gardens: a task so noble and beautiful, a work that has made both them and me a little bit eternal, for the spaces we have created carry a part of our soul; they are like Tibetan prayer flags, inscribed with musings, verses, requests, prayers … and which, when caressed by the wind, thrust their musings and their prayers into the universe, spreading from cloud to cloud, from wave to wave to the ends of the earth.

I have had the great fortune of never being absolutely certain about anything, which has forced me to ask for countless opinions, feelings and impressions on each garden and its details. Thus, from the first sketches to the final plans the evolution has been tremendous.

Each and every one of these gardens has its own soul, but they do share some common traits. One of these is simplicity in both design and choice of plants: sometimes it is just one species that has colonized the whole garden, endowing it with impressive force.

These are gardens that are easy to maintain, and where, throughout the seasons, a "green architecture" remains, a backbone shining through the plantations. In each of them I have sought to create clear, individual sensations. As a consequence, the plans have almost always been modified when translated to the site: reality has imposed itself on the landscape. More often than not, reality has made the plan simpler, and removing things has revealed a force and intensity that was being concealed by an excess of plants.

I have knocked down stone walls; changed the course of streams; modified the landscape in the 18th century fashion; I have done one thing and the opposite at the landscape's behest – gardens with curves only, and with straight lines, and with a combination of both. I do not believe that one can find a winning formula and repeat it. Rather, I find each garden to be like writing a book: something important that we do in our lives. Each one must, therefore, be unique, achieving its own dignity and subtle grandeur regardless of its size.

I do not think that my solution for a garden is necessarily better than the rest; it is, however, my best solution. I admire many landscape architects – and amateurs, self-taught garden designers – who make me see things that I otherwise would not.

All in all, it is diversity that I find most interesting: summer-only gardens or gardens chiefly for the spring and autumn, depending on the time of the year when their owners will enjoy them – virtually none is used all year round. Some seek the sound and presence of water; others scents, or the colours of the seasons, or the architecture of greenery; some become transparent, while others have a pervasive presence; some have ancient origins, and some are brand new.

Above all, they are gardens … just gardens.

Lines in the forest

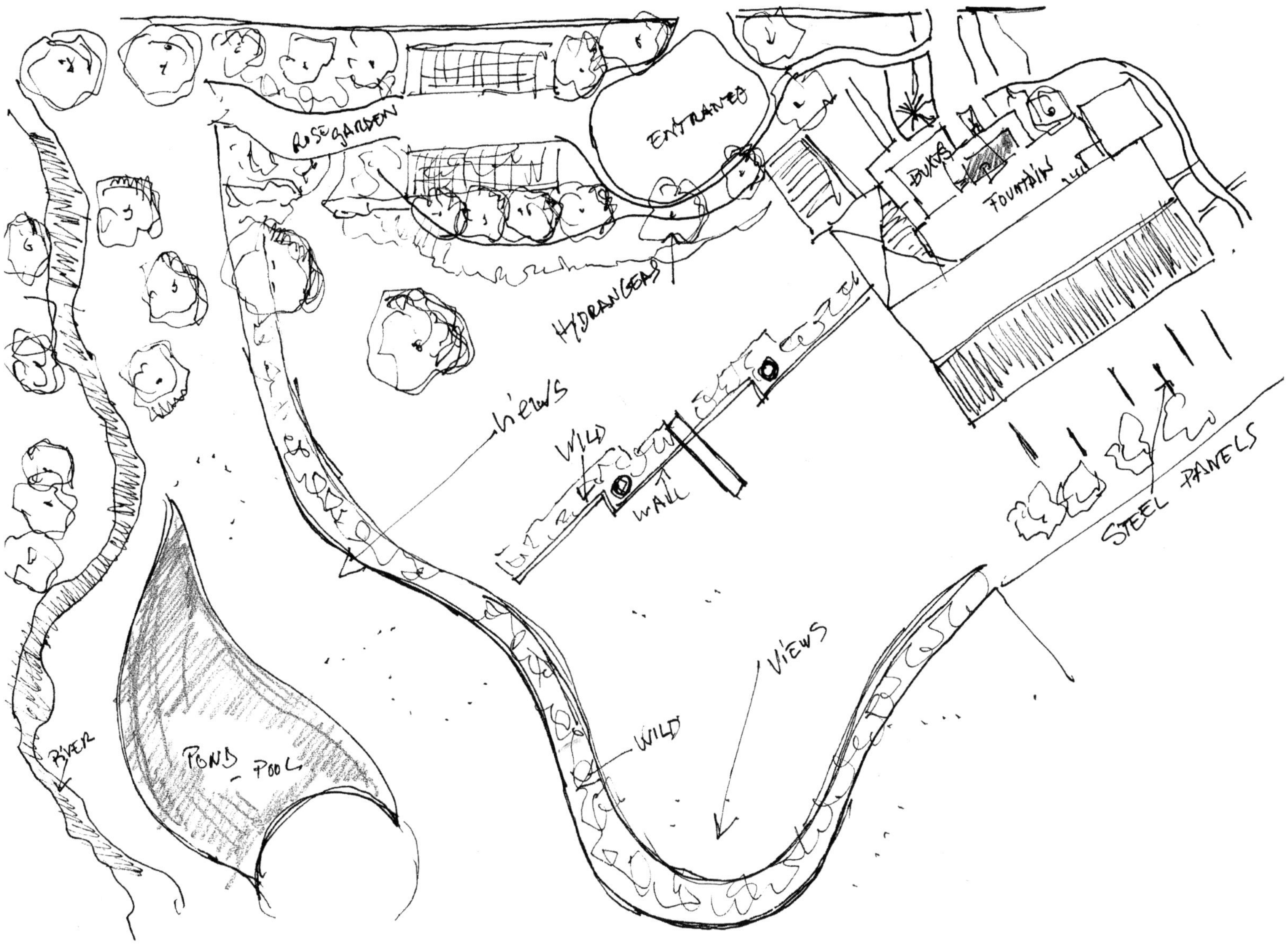

Lines in the forest

When I first arrived in this garden, it was full of walls: a space closed unto itself, devoid of views, with houses towering over it.
However, the hillside, the river and the mellow landscape invited soft, curving lines. I can still recall the first sketches where the hillside was turned into an array of water-filled terraces, each leading into the next, blending with the sea in the distance. In the end, I made only one large terrace on two levels surrounding the house. The array of water sheets became only one, following the brook with a marked, lagoon, or flame-like shape.
The hillside; wild flowers; the entrance; the boxwood shrubs that give an impression of order; ferns; a water sculpture; a garden that opens up as though an entrance hall, while still concealing the rest of the house. An orchard which eventually became a spice and flower garden, and the undulating grounds with wild meadows. The northeasterlies batter the garden once or twice a year, leaving the orange trees burnt and leafless and bringing down larger trees, yet each time it revives with courage, eager to burst out in spring.
Like others in this book, this garden is many people's labour of love. Its owners were the backbone and driving force behind everything; with them we laid out the lake and the trees, and we defined each and every detail, while the interior designer was always taking us one step further. The contractor turned sketchy suggestions into precise drawings … and I stood at the end, drawing and learning from all of them.
A dish cooked by twenty hands, where each added their ingredient.

Previous pages: waves of escallonia and magnolia trees.

In the entrance court, the softly undulating contours of the patches of boxwood and hydrangeas form a highly structured green architecture, while enveloping a modern fountain – the source of a cascade of sheets of water.

Water is discovered as one advances through the garden: it appears and disappears, as though a natural spring. An evergreen structure of boxwood, ferns and hydrangeas is its companion throughout the seasons.

Architecture and nature are fused into each other. The undulating terrain allows for the interplay of volumes and shapes, of light and shade, to offer varying perspectives of the garden – to create sculptural features that change throughout the year.

Previous pages:
The great pond undulates to the rhythm of the ha-ha and the brook coming down from the mountain – it is a grand, organic-looking, perfectly integrated, peace-inspiring reservoir.

The slopes of the woods, sometimes meadowy, sometimes covered in deadnettle (*lamium maculatum*) alternate large trees with small, wild copses. The paths wind uphill through a wild garden achieved with minimal human intervention.

Hydrangea symphony

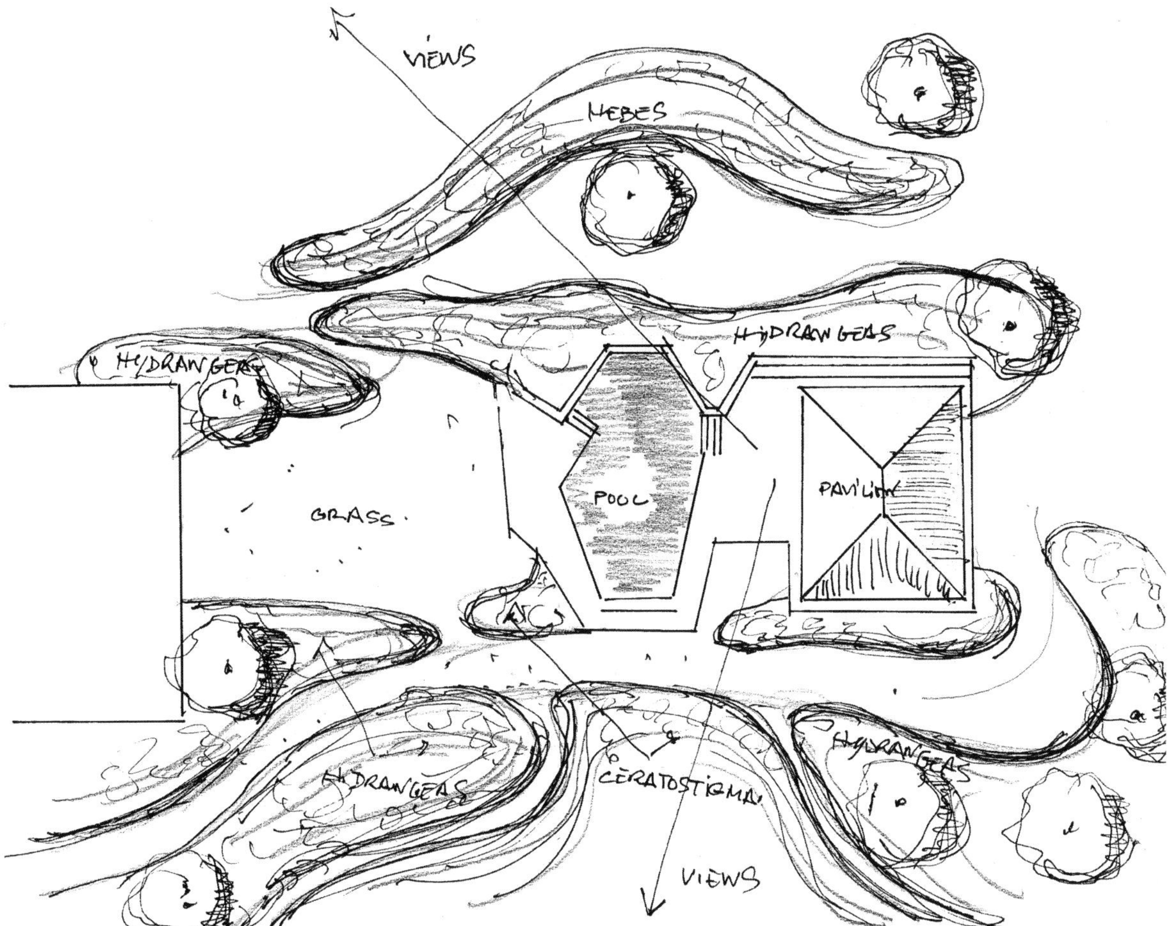

Hydrangea Symphony

A garden for the summer only, using the simplest and best suited flowers.
Hydrangeas are its heart and its soul, shifting in colour over the stages of their bloom, from birth to decay: a sombre and distant beauty, obvious and grand at the same time.
These waves of flowers worked a miracle: they appeared in varying tones – shades of pink, lilac and blue –, a wonder that could only be crafted by nature and soil and which surpassed any imagined design.
Visiting the garden in its prime each year is like wandering through the bluebell woods in England, or the tulip fields in the Netherlands. It is a metaphorical swansong that can be listened to at that precise moment of the year – as brief as the image of freshly fallen snow on the landscape.
It is an ephemeral kind of beauty. Curved lines that twist one into the other, draw closer and further apart, fight and make up, and speak only one tongue, one language only: hydrangeas.
The architecture of this garden is deciduous: multi-levelled terraces of hydrangeas, lead-wort, hevea and a few magnolia trees. In autumn it acquires a yellow tinge; in winter, the architectural poignancy of rugged, dead-looking trunks pointing towards the sky … it could not be more powerful in its simplicity. It is beauty too – less evident but, I believe, of a subtler kind.

Only hydrangeas … large patches of hydrangeas picking their colour out of whim, since they all belong to the same variety, yet range from shocking pink to deep blue. Leadwort and sand spikerush complete the landscape.

Although seemingly contradictory, the beauty of this garden lies in the contrast of the seasons: from full, colourful blossom to melancholy, and then back to life again.

Always the same, always different: always the same plants, but never the same blossoms.

Walking in the valley

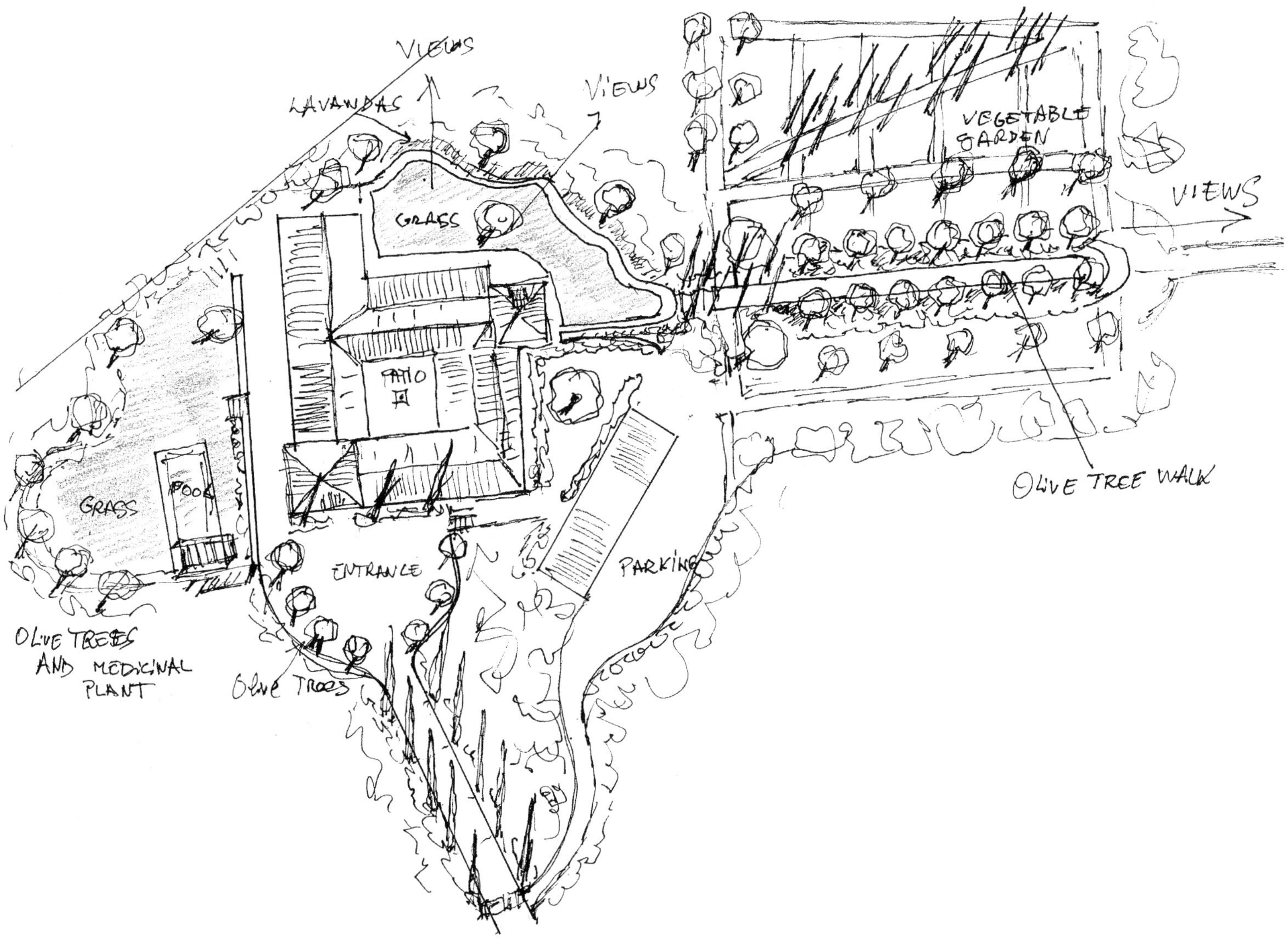

Walking in the valley

In the beginning there was a little house full of charm, and a garden in proportion to its size and architecture. Some years later, the house grew and the garden had to adapt. It began to grow as well, gradually spreading and opening itself towards the countryside.
Toledo, Castile; a harsh climate, little water and poor soil. Only the last of these was in our hands to change, and thus we did so.
Taking our sight for a metaphorical walk, incorporating the landscape into the garden and turning the latter into an orderly continuation of the former – that was my goal.
From the small hill surrounded by a broad valley, the garden managed to draw visitors out of the house and down through the steps and the olive trees and fountaingrass-flanked path, as though olive groves amid the wheat fields.
A small porch surrounded by lavender, Iceberg rose and olive trees forming a slope.
Each line leads to nature: through the garden, out of it and back in again. This is a small garden, seeking to capture the essence and philosophy of what a garden in Castile should be.
Sobriety, character, simple forms.

"When everything has to be limited, the end of the garden must be the horizon." The entrance, flanked by cypresses; one of the courts, presided over by the great olive tree, and the path bordered by lavender shrubs.

This garden always sought sobriety in its choice of species and softness in its forms – both the textures and the tones of leaves and plants should fit within the landscape.

The gardeners' garden

The gardeners' garden

This garden is the labour of love of three generations of garden enthusiasts. First, my grandmother the Marquise of Casa Valdés, who built its backbone: the walls, the steps, the distribution of spaces. Then my parents, the Marquises of La Guardia, who both inherited a great love of plants from their respective parents, and who were keen "aficionados" of perennial plants – highly fashionable in 1940s to 1970s Spain, a fact which guided their taste in flowers.
Finally, myself: a keen lover of garden architecture, of volumes and spaces, of the use of shade to distinguish gardens from one another, and of the structure created by well defined pathways.
In the 1940s work began on the terraces, filled in with soil brought in wooden carts to level the garden. Two of these were formed; the walls were built, and some trees (cedars and cypresses) were planted. The second period began in 1984, when the irises walk was made, the wall was opened and the first pond was built. The third stage brought the second pond and the extension of the garden to its surroundings. The fourth, begun in 2012, created the cypress court in front of the monument, the English rose promenade and the wild cypress path.
This garden has been a testing ground for plants which have later been used in other projects. In some places, as is customary in botanic gardens, it is not only aesthetic value that is sought, but also experience and knowledge.
In other places, that aesthetic goal is taking some time to achieve: we do and undo in search of a destination which is unknown to us, but which never fails to surprise.The garden has gradually opened to the landscape, conditioned by the magnificent trees set by nature in our way, which would not allow us to open perspectives towards the horizon. In a sense, they are there to force us to make something less obvious, more personal and unique … somehow, stranger.

The main entrance, dominated by the culturally significant chapel, is governed by the symmetry of the axis and the cypress plantations.

After crossing the courtyard and the hall of the house, one is deeply struck by the vision of a garden fading into the distance in a repetition of asymmetric symmetries.

The walls and urn-topped pillars bring order and structure into the garden; conversely, the wild-looking patches of perennial plants soften it and, to some extent, break its rigidity.

In spite of the harsh weather, battered by the wind and bitten by snow and frost, this garden has managed to adapt wonderfully. This picture shows the second pond preceding the avenue.

Between the lakes

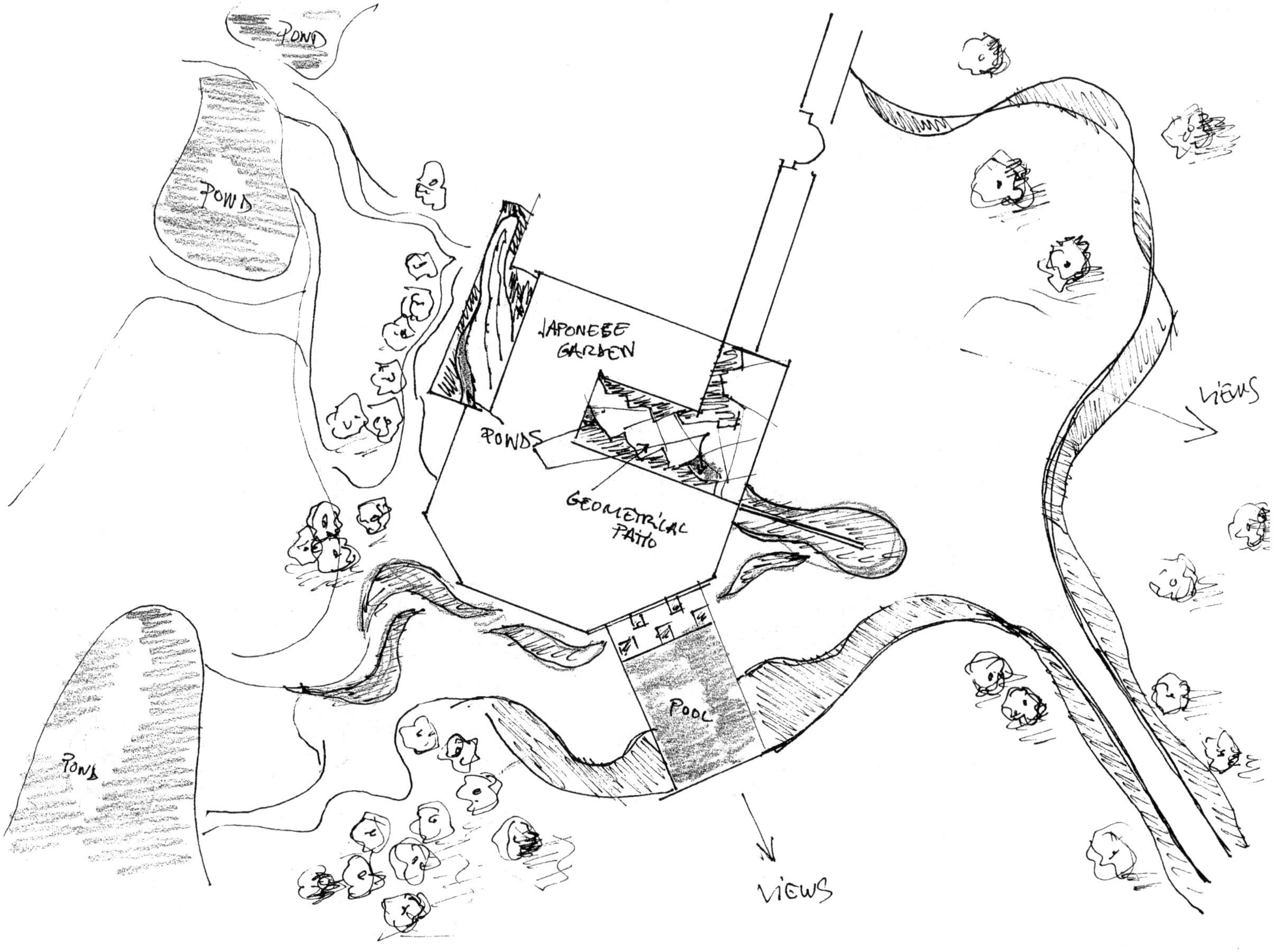

Between the lakes

Between lakes, surrounded by water – yet it was not enough; we wanted the garden to be a water garden, a garden filled with reflections, dusks and sunsets.

One's eye jumps from one plane to another without a breach in continuity, without a single barrier. Reflections join other reflections and recreate a sea in the middle of an unforgiving landscape: water has transformed the landscape, and the garden as well. This is a garden made of many others: the rational garden, with its maze of leaning hedges forming lines that criss-cross and intersect, from which arise trapezes, shades, triangles; and which play with light, water, shadows, volumes, black and white …

The Japanese garden, which is Japanese in spirit only – it is a garden for contemplation, whose soft lines foster serenity and the search for peace, letting the wind transform space by moving the ears of miscanthus and the leaves of the esparto grass – the wind that stirs the water and makes the plants glisten, playing with light.

The garden never remains the same; it invites hours-long retreats – it is a garden for meditation.

The steps down to the lake incorporate it as part of the garden which, in this way, is freed from its boundaries.

Finally, a space with roundish, undulating forms hangs over the landscape, residing simultaneously inside and outside of it. It is a space that refuses to remain closed, and whose central water sheet becomes a cornerstone of the whole garden.

In an attempt to move away from the traditional idea of a patio, with a central "motif" and constant symmetry, here asymmetry is the backbone of the design – lines that cross each other, zigzags and trapysium forms. Two ponds surrounded by escalonia humanize the patio and receive the visitor with the mumur of water.
The strong supports of the pergola are in full view and serve as an additional decorative detail of the garden.

Sometimes when designing a garden it is important to introduce contrasting ideas in order to emphasize the qualities of both. Here, it is the juxtaposition of a classical green patio (500 year old olive trees surrounded by thyme shrubs and a water fountain) with the aforementioned asymmetrical patio.

"The Japanese garden". It ended up with this name almost by accident; hidden at the back of the house, it is a garden for contemplation. The images made by the reflections on water and the shimmer of the grasses rolling in the wind turn this place into a haven, far away from worldly concerns.

There is only one protagonist … the lake. The vision of a watery landscape forcing its way into the garden without permission … the garden becomes transparent, wishing to become a transition – to erase itself. Landscape is the true protagonist.

The lost garden

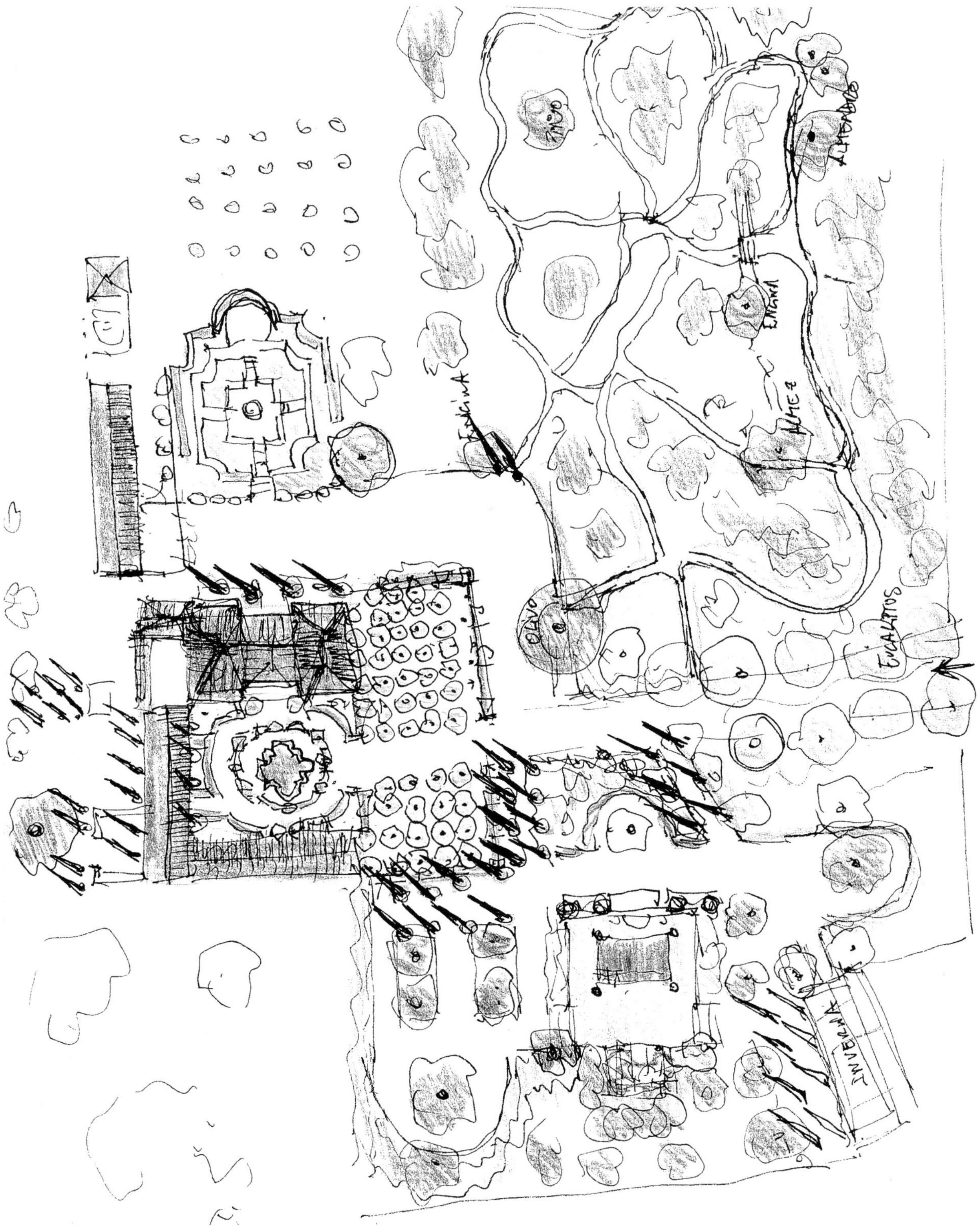

The lost garden

This garden amidst olive groves was created in 1915. The central court was the first part to be opened; followed by an orange grove and a rose garden. The last addition was a wild garden, a waterless garden meant for winter use only.

Andalusia, a paradise of sounds and scents, is host to this veritable Eden, truly a garden within a garden – for nature in this place, full of rockroses, wild olives and jasmines, is a garden unto itself.

In the beginning it was just an olive oil mill; it later became a retreat within a hunting lodge, and finally a family house, where different generations could reunite far from the family businesses. Thus, for generation after generation, the garden has been growing: abandoned at times, yet others – especially in the beginning – cared for with great passion and love: a story of ups and downs over time.

The garden arose from an emotional need for creating, and living amidst, beauty. It was not a matter of chance. It has withstood all adversities, all tests of its endurance: with no water, no soil and hardly any maintenance, plants have kept adapting and have survived to this day in a healthy state.

Recently it has been simplified as much as possible, to the point of closing parts of the garden in adverse seasons, and opening them again for the rebirth of wilderness with the first showers of autumn; these areas are practically a creation of the birds and nature itself, among ancient olive trees and rocks born from the primeval magma and glaciers.

It is a survivor of many wrecks; thanks to the love and toil of generations of gardeners, it has carried on through drought, snow, gale, flood, chill, damp and war.

Its long biography has kept growing year by year, spring by spring, to bring to us a story filled with failed attempts and complete successes; the greatest of these being simply its remaining in existence.

This 1915 garden, designed by Frenchman Georges Truffaut, could hardly breathe – life had been sucked away from it. This wonder of French order and classicism applied to Andalusia was about to be lost forever – yet at the last moment the rose garden could be saved, as could the large, round box shrubs keeping its structure throughout the year and endowing it with identity.

The cistern, made of lime-plastered brick, is now a secluded, secret area in which to remain unseen: the perfect hiding place for meditating among the cypresses, olives and jasmines.

The eyes of Andalusia

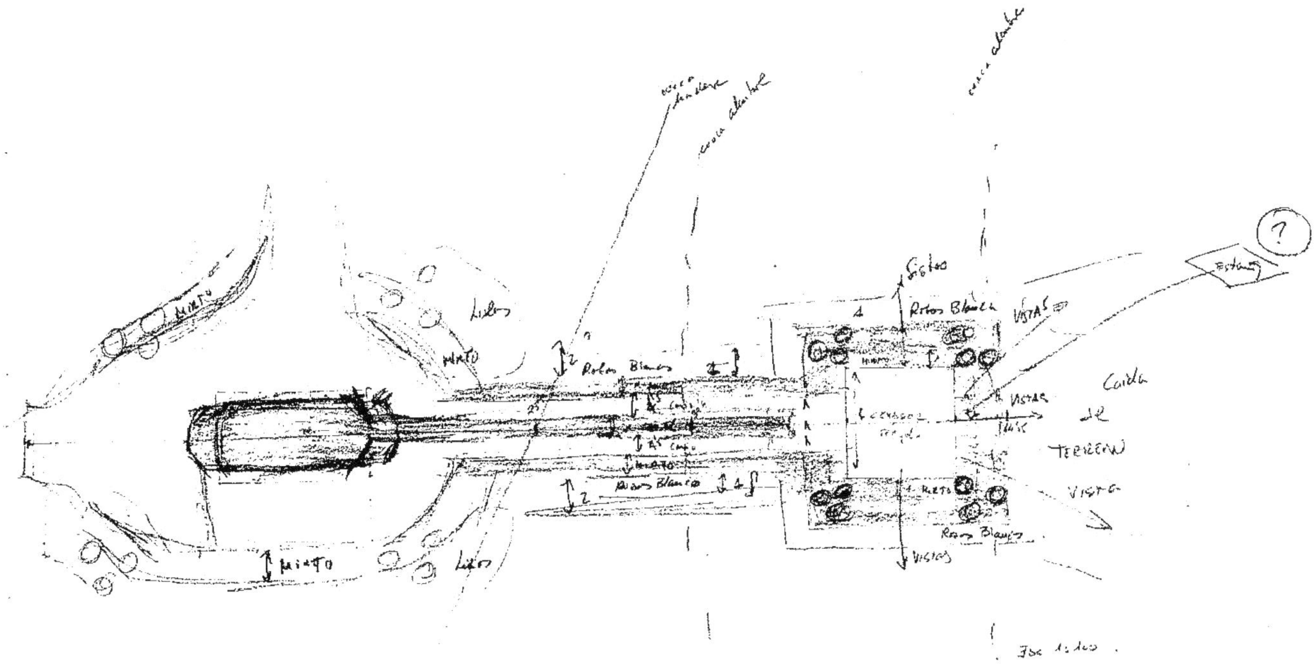

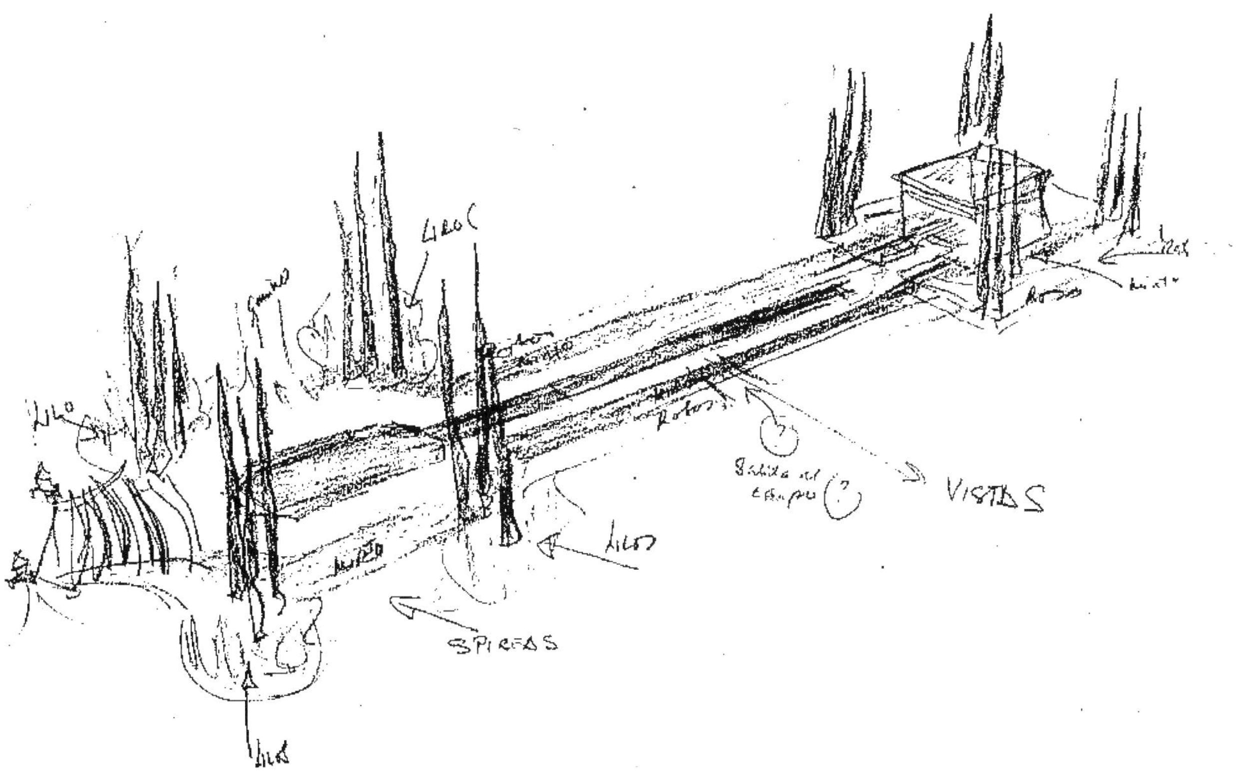

The eyes of Andalusia

I can still recall my first image of this garden: it was a place surrounded by pervasive beauty in all directions, where only a frame and a story were needed. I immediately realised that the display of mountains, valleys and colours before my eyes was too humbling – and soothing – to require entertaining the visitor with visual trickery, petty gardens and flashy shows – these would only diminish its impact. Indeed, the place called for removing, rather than adding – the garden had to become transparent: a garden that would draw one to the landscape and bring the landscape back into it. Shady, elegant pathways lined with cypress and myrtle would act as a mere antechamber, an entrance hall leading to the masterpiece of landscape waiting at the end. We also framed a second picture before a flight of stairs: a pavilion at the end of a myrtle-lined path and a sheet of water: a place from which to see without being seen, set simultaneously within the garden and the fields, feeling open and closed at the same time – a place for thinking, writing and contemplating.
This garden has something mystical about it; something about existing and not existing at the same time, about being there and not being there … it puts into practice the age(s)-old trick of Chinese gardens: through the use of vistas, it integrates elements of the landscape into the garden, thus allowing its limits to reach all the way to the horizon.

A minimal garden of myrtle, cypress and bougainvillea. The path ends before an arbour set amidst the mountainous landscape.

The original, tank-looking pool also has a contemporary character, since it seeks to, once again, make the landscape a protagonist. There are spheres of viburnum and common myrtle, and wild grass caressing the water.

Simple things

Simple things

Architecture drew the guidelines for this garden: straight lines without interruption; stark, compact, massive volumes exhibiting extreme simplicity; minimalism at its peak. The garden had to be thus – the minimal expression of the human hand, like the white paintings that revolutionised the art world and felt more like a philosophical thesis than a work of art. For this garden I had to rid myself of all prejudices, and thus I relied on aligned masses of pebbles, lavender and escallonia complemented in some areas by patches of Iceberg rose and white oleander.
Only two colours: white and green, with a dash of lilac in the early summer. It was a garden meant for spirituality and retreat, a space for contemplation. Rectangles stretched to infinity, narrow, strictly parallel – drawing the lines further and further like a bowstring. Those masses, which in other gardens were curved and embraced one another, adapting to the topography of the terrain and creating soft, wavy forms that repeated over and over …
Here each patch shows its back to the others, becoming part of a puzzle – they are independent pieces that, when joined, suddenly reveal the path that has been walked … like pillars strewn across the field, forming the garden.
This garden has few pretentions; it is honest; it has no hidden depths, no half-truths; it has to be referred to through metaphor and wordplay, for it is too obvious, too evident, too sophisticated to be theatrical – and that makes it engrossingly forceful.
Force is born out of its simplicity.

A rationalist, architecturally conceived garden – almost one more room in the building. Lines spring from the building and are replicated in lavender, pebbles, grass, escallonia and oleander, repeating themselves boldly again and again.

Over the castle

Over the castle

Spread over the ruins of a medieval castle on a vantage point looming over a broad valley, this garden is dominated by history, filled with first-rate architectural features that, enhanced by the presence of pathways, endow it with outstanding character. The garden is meant to adapt harmoniously to the historic architecture, rather than compete with it.

The access, protected by topography, comprises a landscape garden leading down to the castle ramparts; flanked by large oleander shrubs, balls of granite mark the path to the entrance court.

The imposing portal of an old convent presides over the court, while a granite fountain stands in it's middle. Grass beds, white roses, boxwood hedges, promenades, cypresses, lavender paths define some of the other gardens resting on the mountain top.

The garden is, first and foremost, the views it harbours, all of which lead towards the horizon: sometimes to a river; sometimes to the valley crowned by faraway mountains; sometimes to the wooded pastures filled with deer, bathed in the light of dusk …

The garden that surrounds the house is traversed by winding paths and lanes, meeting a succession of gardens along the way that gradually paint the whole picture. It is a vision of the whole through a sequence of multiple images. These dissimilar gardens fit perfectly with each other – just like the architecture, which seamlessly blends medieval and Renaissance fragments. Thus, a landscape garden is combined with a formal court, a parterre garden, patches of cypresses or herbs, that do not clash with each other, but rather add up and create a varied and inviting place. History, in this garden, becomes a past that must be preserved.

This garden, grown over the remains of ancient walls, has turned decadence into order. The great court is preceded by an open, paved courtyard centred on a fountain.

The speaking garden

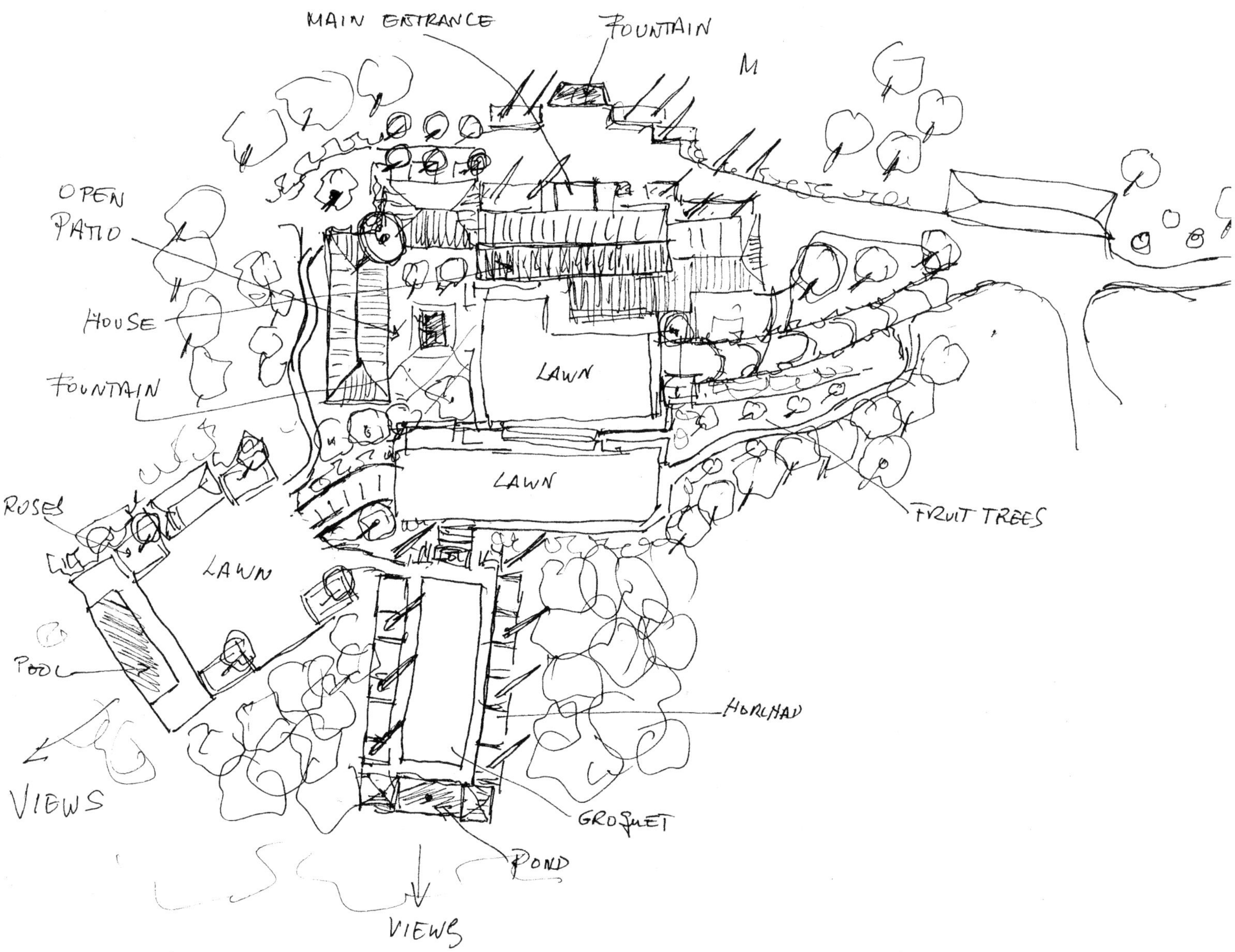

The speaking garden

If there is something unique about Castile it is its light: clear, transparent – an atmosphere wiped clean by the chilly winter winds, which becomes even purer the further one is from town.

This garden lies on the southern slope of a mountain, looking over the axis of a valley that reaches far away, covered in picturesquely composed shrubland and small olive groves – a valley facing west, which aligns precisely with the sunset at some times of the year.

In another direction, the garden looks over the hillside washed laterally by the evening light, becoming shaded and orange-tinted as the sun sets.

Its construction was a work of titans – more than two hundred lorryloads of enriched soil mixed with gravel, of mulch and of drainage were driven across the garden.

On the limestone bedrock, which would not let a single drop of water through, gravel galleries had to be made for the evacuation of excess irrigation and rainfall; over those, soil was laid for plants to grow on. This garden was used as a testing ground for numerous unpronounceably-named varieties of plants brought from the Netherlands, which had never grown in such extreme conditions and which generally fared very well.

To reach it, one has to cross arid fields inhabited only by esparto grass, holm oak, bearberry and juniper.

They are soilless areas, which must withstand extreme winters and endless summers without a single drop of water – yet suddenly, climbing up the hill, the landscape changes, and the esparto gives way to shrubland and then to larger trees. When approaching the house, the terrain becomes craggy, adorned by small, fenced olive groves.

When heading towards this house, one has to traverse arid, semi-desert zones and climb barren, lunar like slopes. When getting nearer, everything starts to change. Shrubland at first, then wheat fields and large holm oaks. On arrival, everything is different.

A croquet field surrounded by an orderly orchard, and water at the end of all the vistas … water for the birds to drink, and acting as a boundary to the garden.

Where is the garden?

Where is the garden?

In the 18th century, Capability Brown stormed into the English garden, transforming it from a formal, structured enterprise into what his contemporaries disbelievingly called "a mere meadow". His was a true revolution – rather, the revolution in gardening.
When they were first presented to the public – in a presumably grand English estate – the guests were left wondering "where the garden was": they could not grasp the gist of the revolution that was taking place before their eyes. For this was a quest for Paradise Lost: a more natural garden, devoid of artifice.
In this garden, just like in those, structures and artifice have been shunned, and Nature has been allowed to invade the garden: the choice of plants – which were sometimes grouped into plantations, and others intermingled with each other – mimicked precisely those that were present in the landscape, running over the hills and vales. Nature has claimed the garden for herself – a stroll through it is not unlike a walk through the countryside.
Just one concession was made: a court of olives and myrtle, separating the house from the entrance path and establishing itself as a lookout next to the house, with soaring vistas in all directions.
Here there was no garden but the landscape: the juxtaposed vales and the horizon forcing their way into the house – a breathtaking spectacle which becomes the protagonist of everything. The garden itself is like the border of a cliff: no plantation should get in the way of the vistas, so everything should be low – nothing is taller than one metre. It also had to be autochthonous, so that after the initial growth period no maintenance would be required: one or two irrigations during the summer and some minimal cleaning should be enough for it to have a healthy, uncomplicated life.
And they keep asking: "where is the garden?" They do not know that the revolution has returned … and it has come to stay.

The dramatic landscape is the only protagonist here. In the style of the first landscaped gardens of the early 18th century, this garden seeks that the surrounding nature invade all its spaces, as though there were no human intervention in it. Rockrose, French lavender and rosemary from the countryside find their way in, invading the spaces all the way up to the house, with the only exception of a garden of olives and myrtle, and a pool that seems to hover over it.

In a village of La Mancha

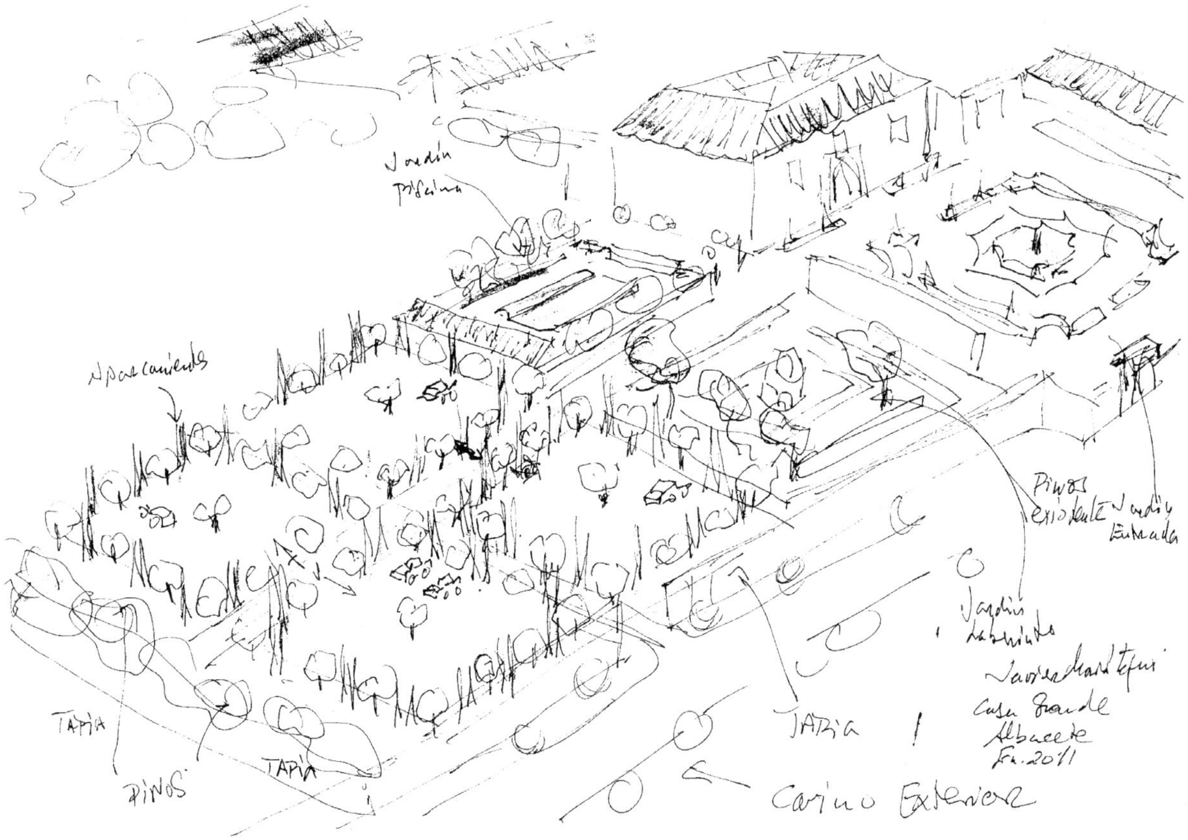

In a village of La Mancha

Endless, shadeless fields, scourged by unforgiving sun and bone-splitting chill, turn La Mancha into one of the most forceful landscapes in the world, which raises passions and enamours, but can also provoke the opposite feeling; a territory which leaves nobody indifferent.

Within this infinite landscape rises a magnificent 16th-century house: austere, stark, solitary, solid, unadorned – a house full of character that defines its garden. The house dictated, as though a guidebook, the design for the garden in its sobriety, simplicity and solemn dignity. The entrance court: a cypress court with low green hedges, a welcoming entrance hall mellowed by the architectural greenery of cypresses. Not a shadow – nothing to disguise the impact of the house. Only green columns on a similarly-coloured base. It is a garden for walking: accompanying and welcoming, but not inviting a stay.

The whole garden attempts to be in harmony with the building's architecture, and thus it comprises very few elements. It seeks light and shade, not colour. From a contemporary but historical mindset, it looks for what could have been, trying to bring back the spirit of a bygone era to its visitors.

It does not attempt to be revolutionary – it just tries to fit the architecture perfectly.

The swimming-pool is designed in the spirit of a Pompeiian peristyle, with water as the axis around which everything happens; like a porticoed courtyard with, yet again, cypresses on a base of escallonia.The rose garden is in the spirit of the Renaissance secret garden: a hidden place behind the wall, where one can see without being seen – the "folly" present in any self-respecting Renaissance garden. Here, flowers, shrubs and water are the hidden pleasure, the small jewel that must be found in each garden.

This Castilian palace, compact, stark and sober, imposes its rules on the garden, which simply translates the architecture into plants: cypress, escallonia and laurustinus, and nothing else.

The garden of a hundred gardens

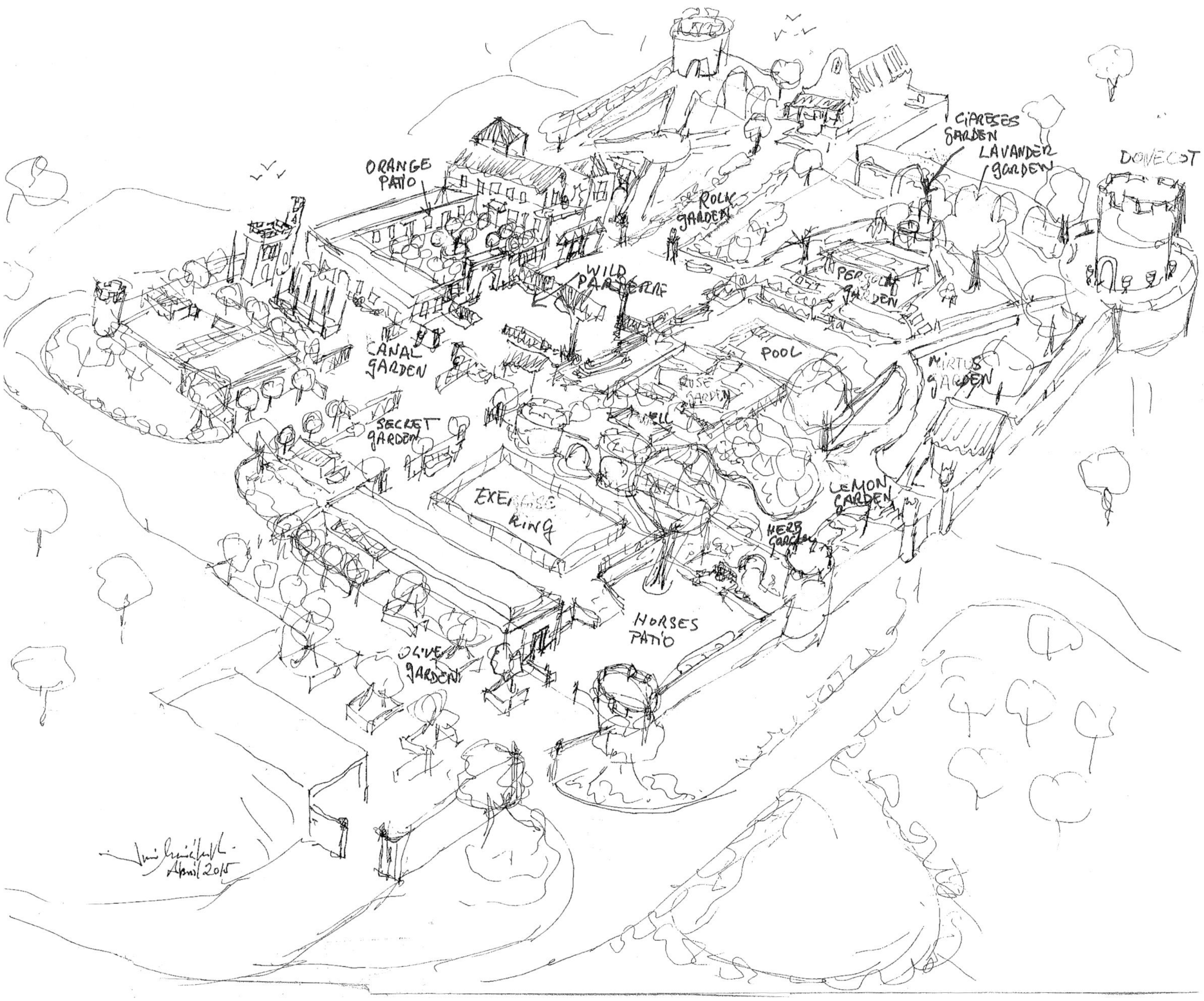

The garden of a hundred gardens

Carpe diem – live the moment.
Andalusia, vital, passionate, whispers in our ear: this life philosophy – this garden talks to us under the scent of lemons, the fragrance of jasmine, the music of water, the perfume of orange blossoms: it has its own language, its own atmosphere.
The garden hides us, gathers us and teaches us how to see its own world: a garden of gardens. Flowers, water, and once again the horizon making its way into the garden, making it infinite. It is the outcome of many ideas and of many people – centrally, the owners' concept, setting the guidelines, though sometimes varying from what they initially wanted; then, the interior designer's hand, the contractor's, the gardener's and, finally, that of myself. The authorship belongs to each and every one of us.
Since the first drawings we have had more than thirty versions – nearly forty – and each one was thought over several times and accompanied by numerous sketches. The garden was not made in a hurry, and it has taken years to make some of the decisions, taking our time until we felt that the choice was the right one – yet once the choice was made it often had to be finished a few days later.
Skimming through the notes we took, the letters that we wrote and the sketches we exchanged feels like reading through family history – like the creation of a work of art, where we have walked the path both ways countless times, to and fro, doing and undoing, for a clearer perspective.
Terraces were created, keeping the orange trees and adding gardens where there were none; then came the riding hall, the entrance court, the lookout on the dovecote, the myrtle garden; the working courtyard, the access lined with carob trees, the way to the chapel, the lemon tree passage, the dollhouse garden … and thus, we have continued to create gardens inside the garden: the spring garden, the scent garden, the wall garden … all under stringent conditions: low maintenance, fragrant plants and the murmur of water. In other words, a garden for the senses: Andalusia.

This garden encompasses so many others that we have chosen to call it the "garden of a hundred gardens". The central orange court is its heart: it articulates everything, with one garden after another emerging from it.

A completely natural rock garden using only autochthonous plants rises towards the chapel. The plants, left untended, have to survive by their own means – the battle for survival is won only by the hardiest of them.

Water in all its shapes: a spring, waves on a surface, a mirror, a basin, a trough, a fountain…

Jasmine, water and shade – the lemon-tree tunnel. Shade, colour and fragrance: it could not be more exotic, it could not be more Andalusian. The garden has become more sophisticated: the more primitive, simpler plantations have been dignified – the frogs have turned into princes.

The towers, surrounded by lavender and trimmed to a curvilinear silhouette, show a mellow, accommodating beauty.

This garden, presided over by a trough of oxidised steel, was inspired by the Court of the Myrtles (Patio de los Arrayanes) in the Alhambra of Granada: a space where sky and "ground" merge. Cypresses and myrtle frame the painting, providing perspective and contrast.

Two views of the trough: as a mirror, and as a set of waves created by a bubble. With the daylight or the sunset these create a thousand shapes that fade into the distance.

Lavender path with arches of royal jasmine.

The sea of myrtle cascading downstairs.

The herb garden. Where the orchard used to be, more than thirty varieties of medicinal plants and cooking herbs were planted. A medieval-style garden was created, meant both for resting and for healing.

The spirit of contemplation

The spirit of contemplation

The Eastern approach to gardening is strikingly different from the Western one: everything is subtler, less obvious. It is necessary to explore fields that are totally foreign to us: a strikingly different philosophy embracing ages-old, yet perfectly current concepts.

A garden for the senses is not merely a photograph: underlying the "details" is the essence of the garden – its transforming force: being in the garden.

For instance, in the East it is not the plant itself that is desired: rather, one seeks the effects of that plant on the environment. The shadows it casts on a wall, the sound of the wind whistling through it or the shimmer of its leaves under the sun are at least as important as its shape or its colour.

Here the goal is not just a peaceful sensation – it also includes the transformation that can be effected on individuals through their immersion in the garden, its imagery and its contrasts. That is the reason why rigidity and flexibility (cypresses and grasses) are opposed, as are the permanent escallonia hedges and the transparent, volatile bamboo. The pavilion hovering over the water is a place for retreat and meditation: it almost allows one to travel to distant lands just by closing the eyes.

Here Western rules do not apply: the spirit of freedom depends more on sensations than it does on effects.

East is East and West is West – and the twain shall meet in a garden .

It is not at all Eastern, or Japanese … but there is a certain similar sensation, or set thereof, when one submerges oneself into it … It is essentially inspired by the reflections and the softly trembling grasses, shining and shimmering under the wind and the sun. A garden of transparencies and flexible leaves, contrasting with the immutable cypresses.

The tapestry garden

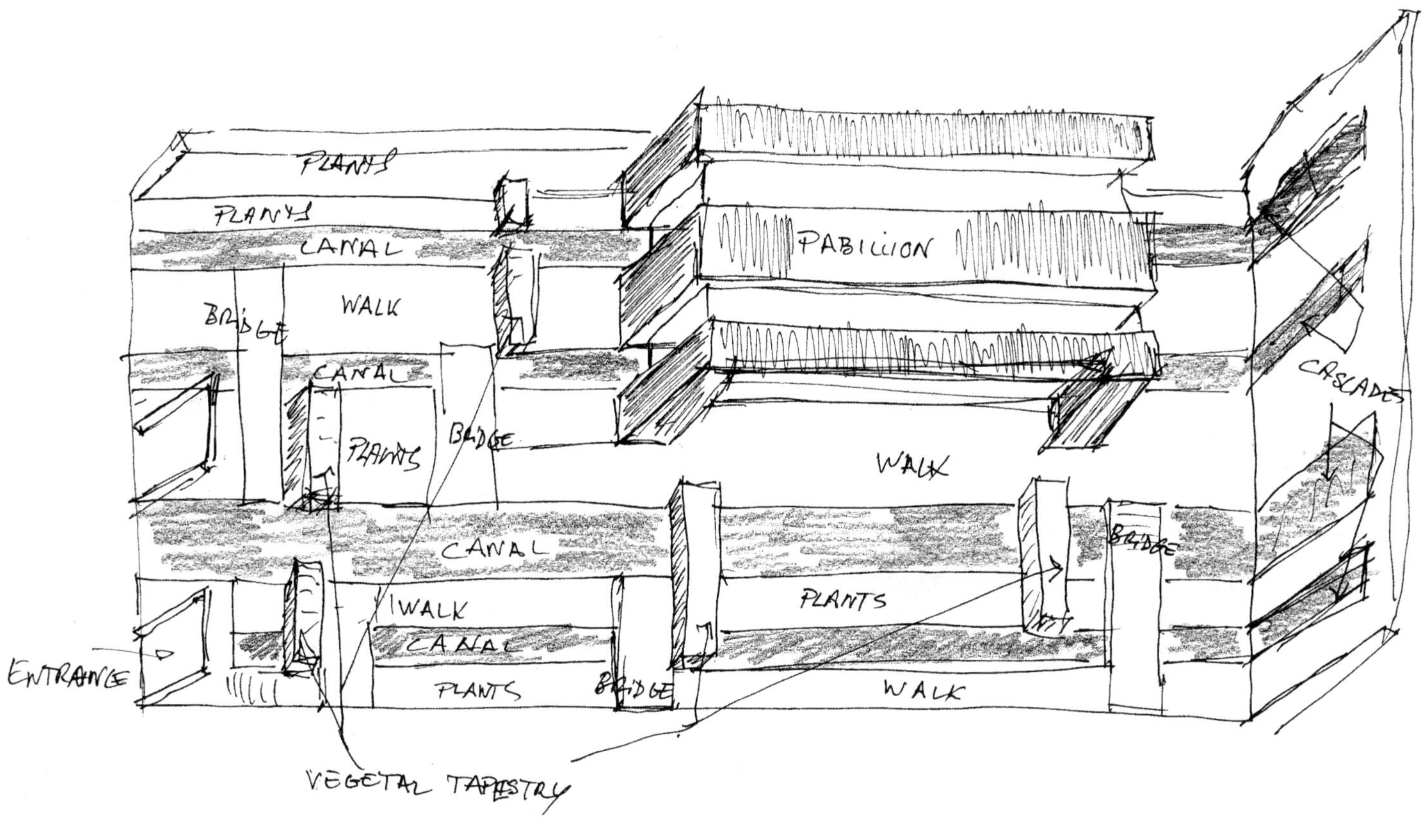

The tapestry garden

I always liked challenges, but when I first saw the area where I would have to design the garden, my heart sank … I was left speechless.

Dark, concrete industrial premises, with a shape all out of proportion. It was more than a challenge, even if I overlooked the slight problem that plants "eat" light; in other words, plants cannot live without light.

Of course there is always the possibility of installing light bulbs all along the garden, giving enough light for the plants to live but at the same time destroying the esthetic values of the entire area.

In addition we had to adapt to several determining factors and regulations; It would have to be an area where thousands of persons would walk (it was actually visited by more than five hundred thousand people)…we also had to create a pavilion for guests inside the garden, where they would be able to see without being seen. All these details contributed to limit the design and compelled me to rack my brains to solve the problem.

The difficulties inherent of the industrial premises, namely a long and narrow shape, led me to take the decision to create four parallel channels which stretched along the pavilion, literally dividing it into strips.

These water channels divided the gardens into long, narrow strips, which, at the same time, gave unity to the entire area. They were a conducting thread which afforded the garden with a harmonious and uniform perception.

I intended to create a labyrinthine sensation, whose shape, with sways, bends, and vertical gardens would work a screens hiding the entire design, only allowing a view of the next stretch of the garden.

After each bend, gardens would appear in succession, crossing water channels and reflecting the garden.

Water would issue as a water source from a vertical garden, flowing down from the heights, whence it would flow along the pavilion in four parallel channels.

The colour of autumn

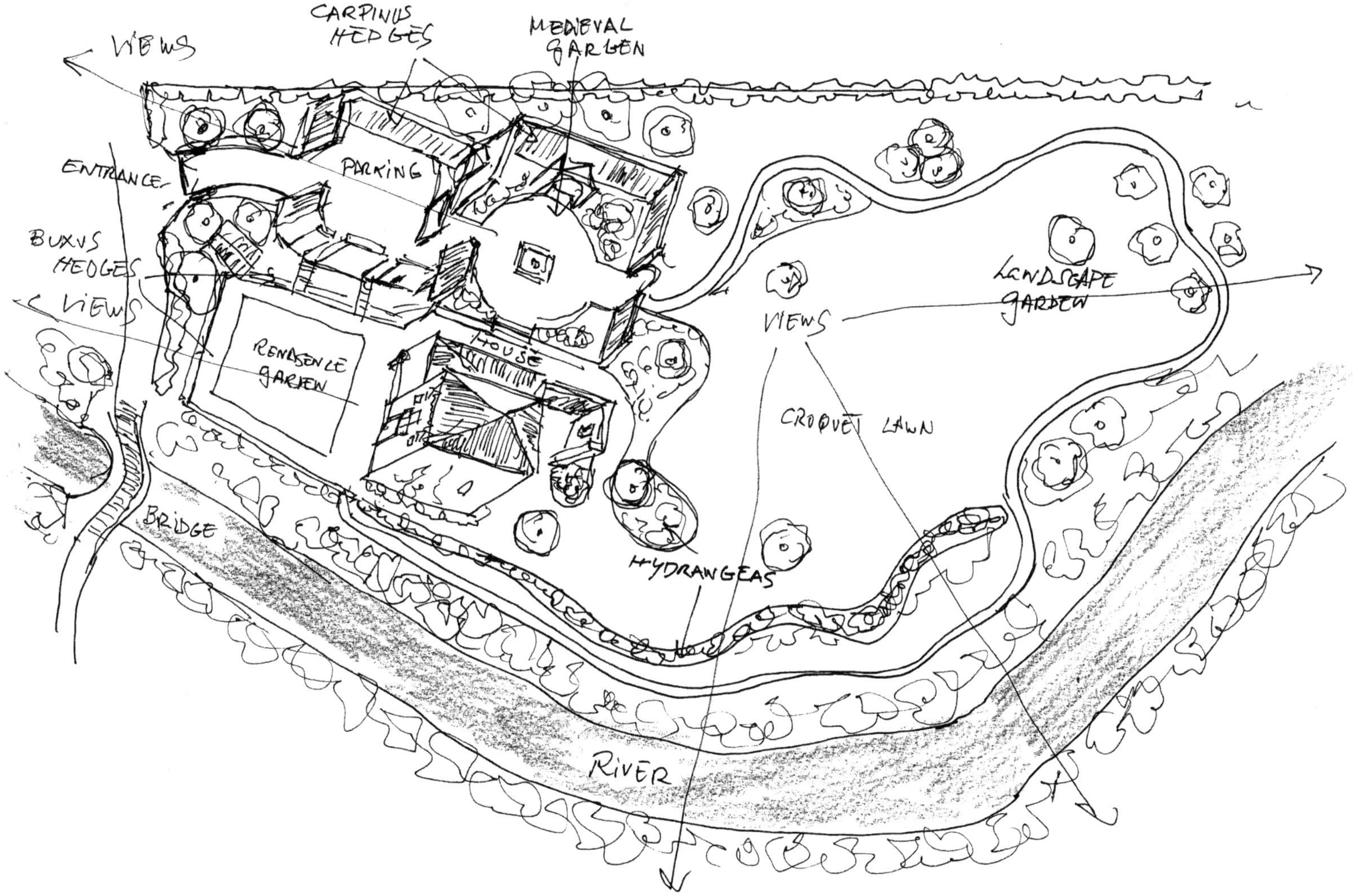

The colour of autumn

When this tower was built the battles between competing Basque clans were frequent, and the towers that stood in strategic passes were the only safe places in times of war. These dark days lasted for centuries and only disappeared at the beginning of the Spanish Reconquista as a result of the Catholic Kings' decision to shorten all the towers in the peninsula, in order to restore authority to the nobility.

In the XVII century, having lost their defensive properties, the towers were turned into residential towers and palaces, with large gateways opened through their thick walls, and decorated with coats of arms, balconies and windows.

As their inhabitants abandoned these towers to live in cities, they ended up being used as grain stores, as mills or stables.

When they were converted back into residences I was faced with the dilemma of what spirit should the new gardens have. Medieval, Renaissance, English landscape, or maybe even a mixture of the three styles?

Medieval gardens were closed spaces, normally square, highly structured that had to be practical and aesthetically pleasing at the same time. They housed vegetables, flowers, aromatic and medicinal shrubs and plants. Symbolism played a major part in the design, both in the choice of plants and in the structure of the garden, combined with images and concepts linked to traditions and religion. Ordered and geometric design was given a divine function.

The Renaissance revives the aesthetic ideals of ancient Rome, but continued to base itself on the ideas of order and geometry in design. English-landscape gardening searched for the lost garden of Paradise and explored ways to represent the ideal natural landscape in the garden.

In this garden we can find the three styles; a medieval garden on the west side, a Renaissance garden opposite the main entrance to the tower and a English-landscape garden that emerges from the ruins.

The Renaissance garden that fits perfectly with the Baroque façade is the essence of the Renaissance; order, geometry and beauty, reduced into a green "carpet" surrounded by shrubs, framed by a gravel path, and decorated with white roses, symbols of beauty.

The medieval garden as previously described, is geometric, closed and intimate. Decorated with medieval symbols, the water in the cen ter is the spring of life, and all around it, in a "hortus conclusus", medicinal, edible and flowering plants.

Finally, a landscape garden is born in the ruins; open towards the mountains, following the river to the horizon. Waves of hydrangea are the gentle point of union between the medieval and the English-landscape gardens. I left the fallen trees, incorporated the river in the garden, created wild pathways bathed in torrential water and finally placed a huge green "desert", surrounded by groups of trees or trees on their own.
The union of 3 worlds in one, like an Autumn day.

FAM

Work in progress